More than That

poems

Anthony J. Alexandre

Copy edited by Nicole Fegan

Cover & Interior Design by Nuno Moreira, NMDESIGN

(Paperback): 978-1-7364499-1-2

(Hardback): 978-1-7364499-2-9

(eBook): 978-1-7364499-0-5

Instagram account: @Y_not_ink

Email address: Tonyinc1@gmail.com

More than That

PREFACE

I have often been asked what poetry means to me. I am always surprised at how difficult it is for me to answer in a way I deem accurate. In order to get a closer view of the answer, I have looked to other poets. I find however, that we would not define poetry in the same terms. If I am honest, in a very beautiful way, poetry is one of the most out of control things I know of. It does not remain loyal to a single definition, and so I can not be expected to offer anything succinct. I do know however that what poetry demands from the writer is freedom. Unyielding honesty within is the beginning of poetry. This book is honesty induced freedom. Themes included in this book are self reflection, faith, musings on love, race, and of course the love of poetry. There are also sections of this book dedicated to justice and the rejection of sex as a taboo. The majority of the pieces in this compilation were written between 2019 and 2020, while other pieces will stand out as being over 15 years old. Some pieces are fiction and others are non fiction, while some are a woven tapestry of the two. I have not attempted to make a distinction for the reader. I will leave it to you to enjoy.

1 True and Dream

Monday

I'd speak to you in melodies
I've written into treasuries
To flood the banks of memory
If ever you'd forget me.

Tuesday

If daily smiles elude you
Then I'll come to the conclusion
You and I need closer hugs
Until those hugs become a fusion.

D R A W N

Drawn to her beauty, so I draw it in ink
Mimic her curves with my cursive
Pen her superlatives perfect as I know how to
Sense her hurting sincerely
I wish to carry her burden
and bring her yearnings she yearns for
so freely without her earning
I was reminded of strength I had heard of but never seen
She so keenly embodies Royal, this humble, elegant Queen
How'd I ever approach her majesty?
Brilliance caused hesitation
Her presence demanded bowing
Her spirit gave elevation
I thank the Father that formed her for genius in his creation
She's art for artists
Her story so worthy of illustration
A ray of light to my retina
and pottery to my pupils
Chamomile to my worries
as I await their removal
Invited her to the altar
quite eager for her approval
Exchanged a symbol of love
that was custom fit like a glove

A couple like pen and page
that this poetry lives on
recording memorable moments
all lyrically as they're drawn

PENMANSHIP

I've always loved your penmanship
your beautyscript
You've always kept it neat and fit
your grammar clicks
there's never need to edit it
Especially when you write to me
and constantly
spell love with an apostrophe
to show that there is more there than is writable
In spite of all the words you spell
the things they tell embezzle all my sense and well
I'm not one obsessed with spelling if it rings a bell
I spell love l-u-v
You really couldn't blame me
if absurd and worded crazy
it's a word you've worded beautifully
it truly is an art
how you show me love through
ink and sheets and punctuation marks
How you take your time to fold with crease
and envelope your heart to me
with plenty quotes of secrets you deliver
And honestly, when I receive
overjoyed and overthrowing modesty
your love is overwhelming and I shiver

My heart gets steady coursing through a page
when your syllables engage
felt residuals continuous for days

IN LOVE WITH A DREAM

And so it happened, and who knew I'd fall in love with a dream?
So much beauty in a person makes the eyes start to gleam
As yours do
And in fact
you have your own kind of shine
Simple perfection to be envied in both body and mind
A glow of stars and, most importantly, the light of my world
Do I thank destiny or luck that I can call you my girl?
Please do say destiny, as luck can turn its back anytime
whereas destiny assures me that you're meant to be mine
And love is tricky too, but truly I don't say it in vain
I love you as I love this crazy world through sunshine or rain
I thank the sky for time with you,
our time is precious indeed
Sometimes I feel my time with you is really all that I need
I value it so much cause I feel It's too good to be true
I rush my time with other things so I can slow it with you.
Sometimes I dream of you and wake to find I'm still in a dream
Fantasy finds my reality and steals it, it seems
But I'm happy in this life it has created for me
So I dare not try to fight it; hence, I just let it be
Heavenly angel, golden halo, still you fly without wings
I thank my God for you, my gift, and hold you high among things
I take a breath of fresh serenity; you calm me inside

Together we're a prime number that no one can divide
And you are beautiful—I swear it by the way your eyes gleam
The feeling's mutual and true; I fell in love with a dream

CRADLED BY THE MOON

Envisioned you in burgundy
Embraced in arms
Embraced by me
And time gets slow
Our bodies glow
While cradled by the moon
Our bodies fit in perfect jigsaw fashion
As we view and share our passions
And our eyes get hazy
Cradled by the moon
Our figures silhouetted by the flame
while sheets and fire heat our frame
Stillness like pictures framed
And cradled by the moon.
I whisper to you "Lady"
That's the name I call my baby
As you whisper to me "Tony"
While we're cradled by the moon
Envision you embraced
my arms clasped snug around your waist
We cannot fall but just in case
I hold you
Cradled by the moon

MORE THAN THAT

I never thought that I could ever feel so far above
and so much deeper and much further complicated than love
And so much stronger, so much weaker
when it takes control
I'm overpowered when it plays its role
And it's not like I don't try to keep it locked inside
because I do I give the rules, it just doesn't abide
And I try to ignore it but I can't neglect
the more I try to hide the more it projects
The feeling I describe is unlabeled by words
and if it is, it's not a word that I've ever heard
So I say "I love you" and wish to take it back
because it's not love—it's more than that
And the hugs that you give, they just make it worse
It's like a double-edged knife. I'm so blessed, so cursed
And I let it cut through when I don't think I should
but still I wouldn't stop it if I could
Because the feeling overall is just so amplified
and I can't find a word to share it so I feel deprived
of a way to show you how I really feel for you
and "love" doesn't work for me It's not enough for you
But then again, I think it's best not to have a word
Cause people say "love" so much that it's lost its worth
So I say, "I love you" and wish to take it back
because it's not "love"—it's more than that.

TRUE AND DREAM

It's casual you'd find me
in this state of True and Dream
where I often spend my time and mind on you
and us I mean.
Forever in this state
with no desire to awaken from surreality
If so, my heart is captive in this place
Unmoving, yet so moved by you
so in you it's an interview
of images and visuals
of us one individual
so, naturally, decisions to
just love you unconditional
build comfort and run rampant in my mind
It's natural to find me in this state of mine
restrained in signs
this love is of divinity and heavenly design
We know it in our deepest heart
and feel it in our spirit
and that pounding in our chest—
trust I know music when I hear it.
I won't lose it
I'm so near it
that I'm in it
and I'm it

And my soul can hold no secrets
I confess and I admit
It's casual you'd find me with our loving candle lit
because this flame cannot burn out in True and Dream.

KEEP

You've halted my mundane
like Amazonian sweet rain
to fertile crescents from deserts
we flourish like evergreens
I've been undone, but
we're fastened together.
Stunned, I've insisted on losing senses
can't help the feeling I've won
All enveloped in embrace
while my heart is giving you chase
I've been tangled in you like laces
to keep my footing in place
honeysuckle, your lips
natural sweeteners to the taste.
My heart is skipping a beat
with the rhythm that you replace
Long-standing love in a vase
knees unbuckled and feeling safe
I envision you in my memory's
corridor that I trace
Unrivaled beauty in bridal wear
my desires inspired
Your laugh is ever infectious
Give all the love you require

I love you deeply
I whisper these nothings
ever so sweetly
I'm walking into your future
where you've desired to keep me
And we'll never be departed
I'll tend the fruits in your garden
I'll nourish you at the roots
so we both can cherish the harvest
In unpredictable hardships
I'll steer you clear of the harshest
hurricane heavy rains
or the stormiest of the nonsense
Securing you with my finger tips
safety inside my hands
and we will abide forever
inside a spacious romance.

2 The Master's Piece

Wednesday

Senses in awe
Handwritten beauty that
never falters or ages at all
Matchless and crafted on Heaven's altar

Thursday

The mirror's an artist
Echoing beauty fluently
Harnessing charm that's disarming
Drawn in the heat of light from the dawn.

LOST AND FOUND

Just take a moment to breathe this air as I'm lifting you up
You feel forgotten while, truly, I've been much nearer than touch
Allowed your spirit to hear me, although it's not with your ears
It's from your inner destructed places, the source of your tears
Daughter I've strengthened you, though you feel weak while
facing your fears
I've heard remarks that you've made absurdly, like nobody cares
As if my kingdom is merely an acre, throne is a chair
Made you a heavenly citizen and I've seated you there
Follow my voice through these ruins. I am the compass you seek
I am your comfort, compassion, incomprehensible peace
The true fulfillment of sanctuary and soundness of mind
and you, my branch can't maintain it unless you live in the vine
Pay close attention—the spirit is crying ABBA inside
Your intuition has told you you're self-sufficient. It lied
I've built community for you. Don't suffocate in your pride
You've been expecting to fly
I do the work, you should glide
The reason darkness surrounds you
Is cause I've made you a light
I've said it's finished, but you're defending yourself in a fight
Told you my yoke is so easy and that my burden is light
and you've been dying while lifting your own with all of your
might

I will not take it if you're refusing to loosen your grip
You won't relinquish the very issues that cause you to trip
I am the peace that surpasses the understanding you chose
Standing beside you. Still waiting for you to hand me the load.

THE LAND I DON'T APPROACH

It's getting hard to believe I'm just a traveler
Especially with flesh being my vehicle
I've given up the keys and I'm the passenger…
Until it reaches speeds I've never fathomed
I then regret my choices and decisions
held accountable like Adam
It's hard to know the Father isn't mad at me
His Majesty accepts me as His only son
but I feel like the only one
who feels as if His Spirit isn't in me
too stuck in the world
I don't love it, I'm just friendly…

But then He teaches me the culture of a Land I don't approach
and I doubted till I saw it in a vision while He spoke
not a village, but a Kingdom, where the King's the Lord of Host
and I can't afford forgetting it
I promise that I won't.

So empty are my words
I speak my feelings
can't swim in this world
Only sinking seems appealing
I would climb the walls to leave my shame
but Sin's the ceiling

Can't run to the Word
not at first. It's too revealing
I feel my corruption legible on my face
Can't feel my adoption, never feeling His grace
Trapped inside a nature I cannot escape
I want the bread of life but something's blocking my taste

But then He teaches me the culture of a Land I don't approach
and I doubted till I saw it in a vision while He spoke
not a village, but a Kingdom, where the King's the Lord of Host
and I can't afford forgetting it
I promise that I won't.

Your love is overpowering
freeing me from my doubt
Rescuing my heart from my thoughts
leaving them out
I'm awed by how The Heavenly God
Can love a "me"
Put worship in my heart again
tell me who I should be
Give me of your Spirit
and let me carry your Name
I abandon idols
and You put them to shame

I tell all the people
how You cured all my pain
They ask by what Authority
I tell them You reign

And how You're teaching me the culture of a Land I don't
approach
and I doubted till I saw it in a vision while You spoke
not a village, but a Kingdom, where You're still the Lord of Host
and I can't afford forgetting it
I promise that I won't
And I live this life abundant
In the presence of your Throne
bright, shining like the sun
rooted, solid, precious stone.

THE MASTER'S PIECE

I wonder what I'd choose to say
If You decided that I'd write a poem for you today...
You'd probably tell me that they're numbered as the grains of sand
Your thoughts toward man are just too high for me to understand
And now I know that I would probably jump to touch Your hem
so not to hear, "O ye of little faith," like sorry men
But then again, I'm just as sorry; Lord, relieve my doubt
I make excuses like there're scorpions and snakes about
I'm way too self-involved, so how can I perform your will
when I can't open up my heart to all your people, still?
Lord, when I'm filthy, would you purge me in the endless flow?
I want to grow mature and follow everywhere you go
I used to think a man was bone and blood and flesh and skin
but now I know that there's a Spirit that should dwell within
Lord, I would call for it, my heart just needs an open door
I know you've given me grace—would you show me more?

I wonder what I would say; give me the words to speak
I stand before you as clay and as the Master's Piece
If I could tell of your love, would the world believe us?
I wonder what I would say In the name of Jesus.

Now, Father, I'll accept no counterfeit
I let the pastor preach but I jump in the word a bit
I don't believe it just because the message sounds legit
I want the certainty that it came from your penmanship
The heathen try to get to Eden by some other way
Please let them know, my Lord, the Cherubim are not for play
You told me Jesus is the only entrance for your sheep
The man who enters in some other way is called a thief
And if they doubt you, Lord, I pray you help their unbelief
No man is righteous; all are sinners, of which Paul is chief
But you have reconciled the World to you and gave us peace
You said to carry up our cross, not just the "Jesus Piece"
We couldn't do it, Lord, we tried and couldn't make it through
We fail with flesh as weak as this. What else is left to do?
But now your Grace is here, I enter boldly to your throne
And say a prayer—Father, if you're willing, make me whole.

I wonder what I would say; give me the words to speak
I stand before you as clay and as the Master's Piece
If I could tell of your love, would the world believe us?
I wonder what I would say In the name of Jesus.

JOSHUA

Then, all of a sudden
He called me from a mountain
Voice was so powerful
wasn't really shoutin
Sounded like many living waters
like a fountain
Moses, my servant, is
dead and he's buried
My word, my law, my vision
he carried so
Joshua, I need you to
build this military. I'm
giving you this vision so
Israel can marry me
and I give you this guarantee
behold I go before you
Every place you tread your foot is yours
just as I have told you
There shall be no man alive
able to withhold you
Just the same as I have been with Moses
so will I be with you.
Abram into Abraham
Look at my integrity
Put the land in both your hands
Ambidexterity

So that it may go well with you in peace and prosperity
commit the law into your heart
all that I've commanded thee
This day in this way
inherit milk and honey
cause it's flowing like I promised you
and Egypt is behind you.
The Jordan is before my people
be of good courage
Cross it over in my victory
subdue the land and flourish
And as He finished I
thought I would diminish
I was certain I would perish in His word.

WORD

I have these words, though not my own I cherish deep in my soul.
I feel they edify like nutrients that cause you to grow
Desired wisdom with no guidance, a vicarious son
Inspired me to be the person that I saw in no one
I struggle with the thought of positive when balance is lost
I feel it's hard to love a gain when we're avoiding a cost
We all made winners of each other
printing currency flawed
Conceited cargo shipped reflections for the mirror's applause
I bring you news of peace that causes wars in chambers of hearts
Misunderstood, though I anticipate the fire it starts
I smile at ashes till they're beautiful. I'll teach you a way
If you let go of bias, pride, and your one-sided decay
Let's rot together from the social bonds so fresh in our minds
Let's watch the thirst for notoriety so swiftly subside
See my perspective like infected wounds you cover inside
I think we're lost inside the confidence we're hoping to find.

DENY

I feel us form into two
We intertwine like a line
from out the psalms
or the creases in the palms
The thesis we live upon
is called love
Often pronounced
out the mouths of those
who couldn't identify If they'd seen it
Condemn it; they don't believe it
Contort it how they distort it
Center it on themselves
and abort it before it's born
Comfort, to those who wear it though.
spacious when it is worn
Only dresses for action
stagnation cannot perform
Nothing to do with merit
inherit it open-armed
Uninvented
discovers our unintended resentment.
We can't present it
while we've been pretending our own investment
Applauding the ones we know do the same

Terrible heretics
Love is like
the dynamite
Big Bangs are made of
Creator of whom
selective amnesia
forgot the name of
Love is the resignation
of all self-preservation
of all your hesitation
to give someone a hug
Or give instead of treating
possessions like a drug
Absolves you of your sin
so you live like One above
Standing before your eyes
though you never see where it was
Excuses: not enough proof of Who loves.

SKYWARD

I imagined I was your cloud
Hovering overhead
to bring you rain that would cause
the nourishment of your pain to finally take effect
To watch you grow
But watched you run
Running for cover
Never looking skyward
So that I might heal your eyes
with cold wet understanding.
I sickened you or I hunted you unwillingly
You were unfamiliar with my methods
You wished me to go away
when I had only hoped
to wash you of the dizzy dust from days gone by
And you never looked skyward.

MORE THAN THAT

3 Affirmations

Friday

I'd bring you flowers
By the hour if your soil needed showers
I would soak between the pebbles
Till your dreams took root and towered

Saturday

I'd bring you rays of solar waves
To set discouragement ablaze
And give you scorching motivation
On the heaviest of days

SELF HELP

I'm inundated with this pain I haven't given a name
Cause when you don't know what to call it, there's no keeping it
tame
Hiding my eyes from recognition. Feel it wounding me more
Forever worthless
If there's a purpose, show me who is it for
I feel this nurture-built resentment right in nature's domain
And what I label truth can easily be skewed as complaint.
No problem loving me, just also have no problem highly judging
me
To feel the love of others feels like more of the same
Rather ignore it or appease them like it's seasonal rain
But when the soil's overflooded it gets hard to maintain
They're planting love in me but wonder why it's bearing no fruit
I walk the garden, an insomniac examining roots
I tear myself apart habitually, confessing it now
Just watch the flow; ignore the gravity that's pulling it down
Bringing it up just feels repetitive
Accused of being negative
Then forcefed all these sedatives
For shutting it down

Like there's a breaker switch for confidence that hasn't been
found
And what's ironic is the lack of it is keeping me bound
When insecurities feel vulnerable I keep them secure
Just spending time alone reflecting helps to keep them assured
It's not depression, I'm just not impressed with what I produce
I can't keep motivating self when I can't find an excuse
It's not a cry for help—I'm arid. I don't irrigate ducts
I just can't help the feeling you think I'm perpetually stuck
It's not humility—that'd probably be the worst you could say
Knowing my personhood intently for consecutive days
I know it's costly for the reader, all this time that we've spent
You'd probably make me a believer
Thanks for letting me vent.

AFFIRMATIONS

Pardon; I'm immature
Isn't your fault at all
I reached for something
you held it distant
I trip and fall
Business as usual
I could tell you some stories
They're full of shame and ponder
all devoid of any glory
I reached for nothing, really
Just a feeling I gather
It being rare, I guess
It made me think of what I'd rather
Probably crazy to you
But it makes sense to me
Gave you a general aerial
of my history
I lacked a kind of love
Never had affirmation
Hated the word itself
thought it countered my revelation
Of the God above
Thought it was self-centered
So if perchance somebody sent it
then it couldn't enter

And that's just where you entered
Affirmations and all
I tried ignoring but
those verbals made me ten feet tall
As we joked about giants
I gazed up at the moon
All the while fearing the morning
felt it coming soon
And now my heart hurts
Because my heart is foolish
You wrote of admiration
couldn't help but read into it
Just as I'm off balance
Can't help this reminiscing
I hate the fact you reminded me
of something I'm missing
And now it's too real
Pardon; I'm immature
Pardon; I'm insecure
Never been nothing more
Lusting for affirmations
Or more the aftertaste
Feel pins and needles
withdrawals mostly In lowercase.

A W A R E

I've seen enough of you seeming just fine
Faultlessly framing facades
cautiously pensive in your demeanor
Selectively helpless
Staunchly rejecting the care I offer
In love with feeling neglected
My efforts often deflected by cynicism
The prison you've chosen
Prisms to scatter
The heated light from the love that you shatter
Misery breaking from company
exchanging furious solitude
for luxurious solace
Aware... caught up in the mood.

FOR YOUR SELF-ISH

Deeper than sea, Deeper than you, Deeper than me
I've carried this burden longer
the strength in my shoulders leaves
I can't cover my face
hands full of heavy disgrace
Leaning for balance but fleeing earth to measure my space.

This year, I will bring to you
The end of all plausible disguises
The disintegration of hiding spaces
The quick drying dew of all your self-concocted safety.
True face recognition
A reintroduction to self—
That is correct.

This year, I have for you
The crumbling foundation of your strange facade
A kick in the abdomen to shorten the breath of your ego
Salt for your ice covered smirk
just in case you had hoped to slip that in—
That is correct

This year
This year, I have for you
The backbreaking burden of proof
A glass ceiling for the conceit-induced claustrophobia in your vast
kingdom of self.

OUT OF BODY

Where can I hide?
So sick inside
There's no reply
The nakedness of an old wound
that can't subside
Will I die again? I'm eager
Tell me when it is over
Prayers hesitate
These bended knees get cold shoulders
Will I shiver so incessantly
and label me depressed?
Disappointment is the garment
my attire gets assessed
My entire whole fault
My desires setting fires
and the smoke won't let me hide
the smell of shame when I perspire
Give me nothing in return
Give me ashes
Give me urn
Read the wages in the pages
fear receiving what I've earned
Someone called it lamentations
but I'm laughing to myself
What a mess I am
repeating lessons I refuse to learn.

I can't catalog it all
organize my slips and falls
I feel pain of broken bones
that on the surface never show
Scar tissue on the innermost
personhood of me
Out of body for a moment
till I know where I should be.

4 DNA

Sunday

Embraces to encase you in
I'm grateful of your placement
In my life. Of all the lives you've seen
You've settled in this place.

GLANCING AT PEACE

In *fact* there I stood,
Dark-skinned, in a corner
self-assessing, tryna antifreeze the winter in my mind.
There was Panic, so Chaotic, and Delusion in attendance
but of all these, I concluded Peace caught my vision.
She was beauty in abundance, she was gorgeous
I was missing out
She's harmless but I'm harmed already
guarded but disarmed
Understand that I was skeptical
In essence, who could blame me?
It was smarter not to let her know the rhythm in this heart
Wasn't in the mood to dance, perhaps
or in the mood for chance
I stopped myself from taking action
but unsatisfied with glance...
I glanced
Voice denied my vocal chords; steady speech and diction
would have flowed if I did think it to
it's easier in *fiction*
wasn't in the mood to dance, perhaps
or in the mood for chance
I stopped myself from taking action
but unsatisfied with glance...
I glanced...
and Peace glanced back.

GENTLEMAN

Black man making history, recovering from trauma
Tryna be the husband, honestly, he's never seen his mama with
What's the definition If his eyes have never seen it?
He can call it what he wants but are we settled on the meaning.

Black man making progress—he's an up-and-coming brother
What's a brother if his influence can't help to lift another up?
'course, you have to chart a course and blaze a trail or raise a sail
but brother, are you bothering if you don't care if brothers fail?

Man loving melanin to elevate his people
cause he knows the country's empty words will never make us equal.
He's restructuring America and tryna push the sequel
but we're never pushing play cause any play requires peaceful.

Dead beat, now repentant, but nobody's here to listen.
And his newly found faith makes him feel he has a mission
They're all locked up in his past while he's been hoping for
deliverance
Cause he can't be a man till he finally gets forgiveness

Single father pushing stroller and she left cause he's controlling.
Said she felt just like a prisoner, an inmate he's patrolling
has a lower view of women, has no trouble just offending them
Says he loves the daughter in the stroller
what a gentleman.

BROTHER

I feel your pain, as we are often dissuaded to speak on such things
Our backs were made to carry and not falter
We were taught to lift with our legs while the ground beneath us
shifted
I have heard your words break upon the sand of expectation
stuck at the shoreline of built-in censorship
I have watched you be destroyed from the inside of the armor
you wear
The armor you were given that offers you no protection
Too heavy for you in the first place
We learned our lines together
"I need nothing from no one"
"I am a source of help and not the other way around"
We were taught to dress for manhood with no mannequins
No readily available examples
Our mothers fashioned manhood from memory
We fabricate what our sisters need
We say we know better while we offer our hypothesis
Our hurt goes unnoticed, so we hide it from ourselves
We claim victory
Brother, I see you.

PROBLEM

Tears forming rivers on an ebony face
The screen is laced with the stealing of black life
from the black-encased
This black body is the officer's hobby
they call it shooting the breeze
resting his knee till the breath of him leaves
with several degrees of pressure while the onlooker pleads
watch him lose his grip on life while he bleeds
The lust for power
He wanted to see him crippled
The coward would have continued for hours
If George's air would have kept him there
If George's heart would beat defiance
while he pressed him there
Shifting his weight to feel the air escape
They put a badge on a snake
and let him slither through gardens
promising pardon
and we just reap the poison he makes
A foolish voice in the background
they want to scream "crack," now propounding
to justify murder—astounding
The last words in his ears
the bystanders convulse
It's revolting
to see ignored the cry for a pulse

Not many moments to go

Hands in his pocket like he's conquered a foe

Will he be George or will he be John Doe

Dead on arrival, the lie

While we just witnessed him beg to survive this

but justice is a knee on a spine

We'll never need to rewind

Keep it in mind

it will happen again

A march viewed as a riot if we dare to contend

God forbid, another issue with two different men

A similar situation, just the opposite skin

I feel the tension; you would stop before I even begin

You couldn't fathom such a circumstance. I beg of you, then

why all the controversy

when I tell you empathy fits?

As if you'd never see a problem with this.

PAYING FOR FREE

On a boat on the sea
cargo by forcible means
dying of cultural cuts
bleeding identity bleeds
custom of entities
holding captive
the masses of we
horribly teaching us "no"
horrible, teaching us "oui"
who is this "us"? Who are we?
Hugging a land we can't see
stumbling earth from a ship
clipping all pigmented wings
slipping on shores we don't journey for
don't desire a thing
but of a freedom we sing
feeling the grip of a chain
mothers all feeling a sting
depth of the pain that it brings
snatched from her baby
the pain resembles
the birth from her frame
choosing amnesia
but she remembers
the vivid restraint
rich in the skin with a stain.

Beautiful hue, but a stain.
Ending the call and response
promptly, they're changing our names.
We invent signals
when we find pistols
for now we are lame
certainly real human beings
couldn't be this inhumane
limping while victory stalls
visions of walking a-gain
leaning on victory's cane
unity bringing us fame
Freedom unfathomed by them
Freedom. We've waited like rain
never been given a chance
nor celebrations to dance
though we beheaded the chiefs
they still had headaches in France
ever since paying for Free.
Penniless, paying for FREE
labeled as "poverty stricken," "broken,"
and paying for FREE
grimacing, paying for FREE
finished, but paying for FREE
First Black Republic
the budget subject to
paying for FREE.

MIDNIGHT BLUE

Look, maybe we can find peace in the morgue
Tears on my cheek leave me speechless
I'm feeling weak and absorbed
and bordering hatred
It can't be overly stated
our hemoglobin's related
The melanin varies
you're filling prisons with daddies
And our communities hurting
this is on purpose, for certain
Boys in blue got that poison for show
and close up the curtain
Import a people deceitfully
never treated as equal
and when we tell you we matter
you say the matter is fecal
You kill our leaders for this
You even stop us and frisk
You called my hoodie a threat
You even choke us to death
Shoot us in front of our daughters
and testify on the bench
and tell the judge it's your duty
and how your life was at risk

This is despiteful at best
at worst it's a genocide gesture
Dehumanize humans
who you are viewing as lesser
Our skin is a target
but you're the one under pressure
You bought us at bargain prices
your conscious is vexed
I hear the Cain in your voice
The blood of Abel's a snitch
You've been a brother to no one
Heavenly Father is pissed
You think your social status matters
when the funeral hits
We picked tobacco, cotton, indigo—
it's keeping you rich
You wanted African minerals
Took our African women
Sampled our African vocal chords
Stole our African rhythm
So this African is spittin 'bout
your lack of repentance
baby, I'll see you in court
that Judgment Day coming to get us
You got the culture in figure four
we refuse to submit
'cause we were made in his image
the carbon copy legit

With years of post-traumatic automatic
making us sick
Let's talk these reparations hesitating
hate to relent
Repent.

NEON BLACK

They got us hating our people
Now, tell me that isn't evil
They paper bagged the complexion
'cause dark is vicious and lethal
This colorism gon' kill us
They started black on black crime
They made you hate your reflection
so that you could hate mine
They got us fixing our nostrils
How I ain't gon' be hostile
Auntie perming her hair
to keep that job in the hospital
The cream on her crop
now all these people want locs
And you can catch them with cornrows
though they'd never want our roles
ancestors were kissed by the sun
then hung for the sun-kissed,
strung up, and lynched
at the picnic functions
I feel a way when this topic is touched
see, my school never spoke about it much
Tried to tell us that the Nazarene King, Galilean,
had skin of a Sistine Chapel European
'stead of looking like the average
Middle Eastern human being

Caught you centering your whiteness

do everything to spite this

We're just tryna hold on to our culture with a tight fist

Tell em how I really feel

I just think you fight this

Somewhere deep inside

I think you wanna be just like this

Tall dark for ransom

When you gon' be righteous?

What a full disaster

What you really after?

I have dreams daily

Of bridging the diaspora

Have our own NASDAQ, NASA, and FAFSA

A whole military

Vigilant visionaries

Check the itinerary.

Let me go

Let me go

Nat Turner, turn the burner high

from medium and low

Revolution on my Mental

like a kettle on the stove

Honeycomb, how it's buzzin'

Hot comb, how it glows

I just had to let you know.

D N A

That ancestry won't neglect me
I rub my inner cheek with cotton swab
while the irony is eyeing me
I pay it no regard
'cause the options I'm afforded
will help me get my sullied past sorted
I heard we made the colonizer
soil all his garments and vomit
he couldn't tell a slave from a sergeant
so when they say we're francophile
I really just ignore it
Kreyol is francophone
but they stole us from our home
Little Haiti is a side effect of ships they still own
They've been salty from a revolution
can't leave us alone
but I heard we from Benin
and I heard we from Togo
predated bondage
predated cargo
We should throw a homecoming
reunite me, I'll go
see my face in kinsmen
know it's been a while, though
they tried to kill our culture on that overwater carriage
Changing our complexion and it wasn't love or marriage

Violators violated us. We got divided
When we got together in the streets
They called it riot
They've been tryna act like we're some guest that they invited
Labor from a hostage; we don't even like the climate
Are those founding fathers or some cold blooded pirates?
Our irises tell us no lies—they are violent
Policing all this melanin but burn from ultra violet
Disrespect our women 'cause you want to get inside it
Your day of independence isn't cause for much excitement
I'm waiting for the day you get indicted
I think I'll let the listener decide it.

5 Pen and Paper

Monday

Shelter safety and solace
With unintentional modesty
I'd be lost in your gaze without rescue
If you'd acknowledge me

Tuesday

Dream of seamless connection
Requited love in reflection
The motion of light that moves me
To warm you in this affection

THE ANTIHERO

Who can write this and
candidly capture crisis?
Admittedly omit details
decidedly indecisive
Unfettered, he tells attainable
memories, unexplainable,
riddled with my emotions
like currents subvert the ocean.
You shouldn't hope to follow me close
I've been evading the truth
it's too invasive
the proof
All my relationships
suffer from lack of heart
extract art from altercations
then brainstorm for causes
The parchment needs hydration
Muses leave me enthused
like the booze on vacations
or cruises or clocking out
On the eve of celebrations
Claustrophobic when quiet
escapist when I make statements
The Antihero, "Calligraphy"
shrouded in Paper Capes.

A writer, before I noticed
that speaking was worth a ponder
Could never focus my thoughts
while a rhythm forced me to wander
A fluid flow of intuitive
truthfulness that I squander
on loose leaf
or Microsoft Word sheets
that I'm fond of.

DABBLE

Pardon if I dabble in the arts
nothing dark
I just synchronize this melancholy pleasure with my heart
Telling truths that have been housed
up in my mouth but climbed the roof
evidently speculating
about ever finding proof
of adoration for these words
before they ever get ovations
People think these trains of thought
are always set on destinations
I'm content if they pitch tents
and hardly ever leave the station
never to arouse a reader
or be echoed in a theater
they stay chambered
where the Lub and Dub
and ventricles do lead them
Circulating in the writer
where the writer can't delete them
Sure you understand or empathize
these visions of a hoarder
or decisions out of order
or selective mute of sorts
I'm convinced a pen and wrist
should script abundant smorgasbords

With fluidity untangled
never through a brute force.
Till it's effervescent
with the weight of
lunar crescent
not the pressure of suggestions
never art for sake of art.
Fear of words forsaking
penmanship
and pen forsaking heart
is the reason
I can't finish writing
things I never start
Have me pardoned
if I dabble
No one anchored
can embark
I just synchronize
this melancholy
pleasure

PEN AND PAPER

Dear God, man, we're talking. I'm not shaken up, just nervous
Just thinking to You *thank You for providing me that service*
That favor to be able to just transmit my feelings
through the ink of a pen that records it on the paper
And paper tells the world, tells the minds young and old
who receive it through their eyes and translate it through their soul
which inhales it so they taste it and relate it to their lives
and they feel it and the feeling shows. It flows from their eyes
They see in order to connect these words. I really try my hardest
and I get them from my heart, the true meaning of an artist
When woe is me this poetry is music to my soul
and I thank You, One in Heaven, this is all in Your control
I received it through Your blessing; You invested it inside
it stayed true and so I kept it sacredly and let it rise
You gave it to me so, to guide me through the struggles that I saw
and it also guided others who've reflected on it more
This powerful infliction pushed the boundaries of my mind
Life I'll never ask your meaning, cause it's my job to define
And I'll never hate the rain because the sky deserves to cry
we all get comfort when we do it
Sky gets cursed at not to do it
I'll continue with these lessons cause one of them might save us
and I'll get them from the blessing and the gift Pen and Paper
Along with Music, Pen and Paper gave me poetry. I use it;
God I fell in love with poetry. Please help me not to lose it
Poetry's a constant smile to me when I've no reason for it

but rhyme and reason shines to me, so truly I adore it
It helps me face my troubles. Trouble grows when you ignore it
so I release it through a pen and I grow stronger for it
Readers strengthen, too; they view their broken hearts up on a
page
and it helps to know that someone knows the feelings they've
encaged
And so poetry's my duty and with honor I shall take up
A Pen and hold it in my hand to scribble on some Paper.

MUSIC

Instrumentals stuck in temples
part angelic and muse
Steeped her in water like she's oil
in my leisure diffused
We talked for hours, I devoured all your elements cold
You took my breath on all occasion, deeply touching my soul
I'd tell you things I wouldn't share unless you carried me there
upon your tempo, kept it simple, matched my flow to the air
My one accessory a treasury of melodies taught
with simple energy, I pleasantly pick memories caught
To soothe a mood
a natural remedy
when life felt like a penalty
to battle back these attitudes
whenever distraught
You had me dancing in the mirror tryna lunar this walk
Or singing into fans before the auto tune ever talked
You educated me with Lauryn, an intuitive spark
You gave me Marvin Gaye to wake my city shaking its heart
And then you gave my sister Monica for one of those days
Oh yeah, The Fugees—man, that crew made me so proud to be
Haitian
Especially when we felt like the butt of the nation
You were my light in dark situations
Gave me a knack for creation
A little wrists, innovation

to take a motionless pen
filled with emotions for tracing
although the rhythm of memories
gave me tremors and quite a few new dilemmas
you always powered through the endeavor
How many lives have you saved?
You're always breaking a chain
You're always robbing the grave
Don't think you'll ever degrade
Don't think you'll ever behave.

TRASH

I need a mind that's
Dressed in scripture
When I get scandalous
I need a fixer
Crush that truth up
Make me an elixir
Sometimes my broken situations
Make me richer
Richer in character
But I be acting up
I love to put myself
Inside these handcuffs
I'm gonna snitch me out
Lord, is this court in order
I gotta let it go
Like an imperfect hoarder
This poem is trash now
Pen collapse now
Heart caving in
Mind spazzing out
I think it's beautiful
The pain is lovely
I introduce myself
I meet another me
Sometimes I'm scared to death
They tell me not to be

I pretend to listen
They haven't heard me
I need this surgery
Wake my conscious up
This poem is trash now
Listen how I give it up
I like to put myself
Inside these handcuffs
May I approach the bench?
I hardly stand up
This is residue
It's residual
I tell it, *haunt me not*
But it continues to
I'll probably post this up
Sometimes I feel I'm stuck
What is this writing for?
I gotta spill my guts
I'm beating round these bushes
Like putting trash out
My pages is smoked and sooty
This poem is trash now.

WORDS LEFT BEHIND

Ain't about them adoring me
long as they know the story
Mama taught us to daydream
we never had time to sleep
Never say never
Misery couldn't last forever
I gave my penmanship practice
to contradict stormy weather
From hoodie jackets to parkers
I couldn't afford a blazer
I fell in love with a beauty
and let my lyrics embrace her
Remember me still
though I had traveled
in mixed company
I had focused my heart
on a singular piece of art
Felt enchanted while with her
I withered inside without her
I scribbled on scrap paper
she turned it to a Monet
Lit up the pitch of ink
like the dawning of coming day
She provided a home
for imagination to stray

Or we embarked on a voyage
on which I ventured to stay
Needless to say
Poetry is my messy apartment
had a way with my words
like a hieroglyph on a parchment
The only thing I looked forward to
causing me to look back
on a life riddled with
critical elements that impact
Elephants in the room
I had allergies to the ivory
I made sense of complexity
written in white and black
Forgive me, it still eludes me
the future is still confusing
These words I leave with adhesive
for images that I lack.

WRITER'S BLOCK

They're wondering when I'll ever
get over this cloud I'm under
I scribble drizzles
They miss when the words I pondered would thunder
They've resonated with cadence
emotions soaked their bifocals
The thunder would pound a rhythm
they'd find themselves lending vocals to
Words eloped with their heart
in a way few others could hope to do
Settling for the veterans tethered
to writing regular.
I would penetrate sheets
with the ink of my innovation
the maturation of "normal"
my formula was informal
I formerly did this fluently
pardon my use of jargon
Now it seems that I haggle
with words that offer no bargain
Hindered writers are halted
blockaded writers feel broken
castrated penmanship never
this pen will never quit stroking

A L I V E

Wrote you this message as it exited the right of my chest
with calm composure I've been over all the carnage and stress
went back to writing since your back was turned
The Carpenter's will
Made an investment that alleviated ink from a quill
I searched for mastery
He made me practice patience with skill
Talent is hazardous when emptied with no purpose fulfilled
I had a dream that dissipated and avoided my stare
evicted hope from me and left no vacant rooms for my care
Guess I was influenced by smiling faces making a change
They called it tribal, I got disconnected thoughts rearranged
And switched my focus back to setting all these Post-it's ablaze
I feel Alive again
That comatose was only a phase

AUDITORIUM

Verbally interject
and appeal to pupils with sense
I mean, iris, corneas, lenses
in love with ink I dispense
they're involved with volumes I've measured and want this art
with a tether
so they can take it wherever, whenever, in form of letters
or dressed informally; casual use of poetic license
and auditorium glory if ever it hits a mic
or if I ever recite this
they'd feel a temperature spike
and be cozy, comfortable, conscious
and chill as ever in spite of it
we can make a good night of it
Starry, too, like Picasso
I Da Vinci on syllables
so in love with staccato
smooth on pallet and drinkable
reminiscent moscato
and give your hands a concussion
for going hard on the bravo.

VISITING HOURS

She played me music on an instrument I really couldn't name
and though everybody knew her, she escaped from all the fame
and I asked for introduction but she wouldn't give her name
she just played a higher octave and it muted all my pain
and I held myself together for the fear that I would change
she did damage with the melody. My efforts were in vain
and she painted with her music, with no color, not a stain
just legato with vibrato resonating in my frame.
I was frozen in her chorus
and she kept me in position
and I felt that I should leave
but never followed my decision
and her volume made me nervous that someone would stop and
listen
and be frozen as I was, with me at fault for their condition.
But she cried to me like I could offer freedom she was missing
and I shook my head with frustration freeing my position
finally leaving with a guilt that dwelled inside my intuition
and a burning question;
How could I keep poetry in prison?

INK OIL

Look how they clamor
for royal poetic grammar
to touch us artists
these narcissists
harvest what we discard
Bizarre
Manage advantages
over their full facades
and turn these fakes into fans
for that metacarpal applause
Ink is oil embedded in melanin-covered soil
It's why they need to break skin
For this rich deposit they toil

6 Fractions

Wednesday

Shadow and light
Polar but heated opposites
Smooth gravitational flight
Borderless beauty focused and captured

Thursday

Photo finish
inciting a pulse to be indecisive
Camera-shy, coy but priceless
On image-taking devices

THE LIAR

Although I'm sure this conversation
isn't likely to occur
I've been rehearsing like we lived it
Like it's rightfully a blur
Much like a memory I wince through
When the image is in view
Behind my lids
With careless verbal cues
And body language too
Corrosive counterarguments
It's hard to miss
If looks could kill
Or better yet if looks
Would leave us clutching
Secrets soon revealed
Prematurely
Threats of surely
Shedding
All we hold
Securely
Insecure for
Reasons palpable
Your glance a steady scalpel
Surgery upon my perjury
This injury is murderous
No mercy for the

Liar and his words
You sentence me
Before the chance to try
Me in the court of
Confrontation
This unlikely conversation
This incessant hesitation
This reluctance was the only
Balm I knew
Reinforcement of the
Torture of the thought
Of talking through.

L O V Ê D

I felt your presence in sentences and in nothing more
I felt your felony in me
I felt accused indoors.
What an intrusive confusion
Although I love it dearly
I flee for life though I want it near me
I'm weak and weary.
A whisper crisper than any sound that I've ever known.
A cadence, rhythmic and gifted
Infatuated with it.
A flawless formula, beauty with pull of gravity.
I rest my pen on the frozen ice of causality.
Beyond expression, beyond the depth
Of a single breath.
Deeper than sleep on the lower deck
Of a vessel stranded
Flow unrequited and disconnected
And empty-handed.
Beyond belief
With a joy
That promises grief

FRACTIONS OF MY LOVE

The days I made you smile
The nights I did the same
In youth, I drew those hearts
encircling our name
Those were just fractions of my love.

The times I stopped your tears
and said they wouldn't stand
The day you gave your heart
the days I held your hand
Those were just fractions of my love

The days the skies are rainy
My comfort's always there
The days you're not around
Those days are hard to bear
Those are just fractions of my love.

The day the ring was shown
It caught you by surprise
The smile was on your face
The joy was in your eyes
That's just a fraction of my love.

The night I wasn't home
That birthday I forgot

You spent that night alone
Those tears I didn't stop
I'll make up those fractions of my love.

I wasn't home again
That night the baby cried
You almost lost your dad
Your father almost died
You didn't want fractions of my love.

I was out too long
So you came out to get me
I say you saw it wrong
'Cause she was kissing me
You didn't want fractions anymore
I don't blame you.

Those tears I hated came
Please settle down, my bride
You asked me for her name
And no more lies this time
You found out where those other fractions were.

You slapped me in the face
I know I made you mad
You took my son aside
Told him he had no dad
'Cause he should get more than fractions all the time

Those tears came back again
But now, not to your eyes
How could I be so dumb?
Those tears, they filled my eyes
I lost the two most precious things—my loves
I don't blame you.

"ROUGH DRAFT"

I knew you'd do well
Wishing you well was more a formality
Casual speech for those who really had nothing to speak of.
"Over" was hard, but freeing for both of us
I had hoped for us that we'd see the necessity now
or maybe later
I grew much and more while feeling alone
when in your company
Catching a mood that halted my speech
I couldn't speak
Felt you needed advice from somebody who understood you
so I refused to stand under abuse
I gave you love that I mustered
while I had trusted that you would see my investment
and pay it forward with interest
but you were never that interested
It seems you sought a change from your past
Was I redemption?
Meant to help you stomach your own reflection
sick of your former self
While I had dreams of bringing you health
in no small measure
Truly robbed myself to make you feel treasured
You lacked capacity
and wouldn't keep compassion for me.

Dwelt on it barely, I swear.
Think of it rarely.

IF SHE LOVES ME

Never sure of my feelings
unless my feeling is sorry
This mansion of love accessible
but I stay in the lobby
I'm insecurely unsure
of the potency she denotes
I mean all I have is her words
and so I recite them in quotes
And when I do, I get choked up
the vocal cords in my throat
they loosen as they produce for her
words I say that she won't
This love is brittle and blisters
a heart that's battered and broken
This invaluable sentiment
that refuses all tokens..
My offered, open-armed gestures
I figured we'd be eloping
and wedded happily
I feel indebted with all this hoping
Lay my head in forgetfulness
focus on sundresses
And when this loving is worn
I'll settle for undressing her.

CONFESSION BOOTH

Pictured yourself your own assailant; babe, you demonize love
criminal gestures I divested till you'd legalize hugs
worked to disarm your own assessment so you'd share in my view
How can a soul be bold alone in truth? What's braver than two?
I volunteered to commandeer the work demanded of you
We lifted curtains so you'd have the chance to savor a view
Not that I thought that I'd be strong enough, but thought that we belonged
I tried to right our every wrong, felt we had nothing to lose
Till, very suddenly, you acted like you needed to choose
Doubled my efforts but you claimed that I had nothing to prove
I wouldn't violate your wishes to the sound of broken dishes
felt you ripping out the stitches that were sewn into you
I held my distance for a moment that evolved into few
We changed our status. I kept at it; my involvement renewed
And every night, my Adam's apple
spent the night in Evening's Chapel
praying that you'd learn to grapple
with the battle in you
My love is stronger than those sleepless nights you keep to yourself
I think you love me just as strong. I need you sharing the wealth
I sure had hoped to give you visions of for better or worse
with some delay, I just replay the scene you help me rehearse
I washed my hands and donned the scrubs when you had need of a nurse

when you were parched with panic, I was there, relieving the
thirst
I'm clocking in again; this love is my professional gig
Till you accept my ring, I have no more confessions to give.

7 Sweet Chaos

Friday

Make sensual the science
Like an energized appliance
Get the plug into the surge protector
Legs would shake defiance

Saturday

Love would be the currency
No forcefulness just urgency
I'd bring it to you currently
Concurrently and earnestly

METAPHORICALLY SPEAKING

Metaphorically speaking
It's like you've been plucked from a "Something Tree."
Bathed in a cherry, sweet
Juicy like nothing else
Softer than a melody
played on the black and whites
Backed by a bow and string
Hummed by the elderly to the youngins snug and sleep
Mississippi, how you're deep
Stencil, how you're nice and neat
Heavy on the chest of me, then show you off like jewelry
Hidden in the view of me, then wonder if they all could see
Blink never if it means that you would be a loss
I know they couldn't know the cost, and so
You're meant for me, of course, but, see
I keep you in my present past
You're frozen in my memory
Butter? No. I can't believe it isn't
Smoother, better, see?
Flavor; no description but my taste buds in love.
I'd plead guilty if it stood to mean
That you would be the sentence seen
If you could be my waking morning, afternoon, and evening be.
And I would be in love with thee
Forevermore, so gently
Preserve your smiles intentionally

Your presence is a blessed dream
And all the things you do to me
I can't explain them fluently
No awful things, just joy we see
Although you hid some tears from me
I know them; that's my fear for you
So when those tears appear to you
Just share them in my company
And I'll bring comfort near to you.
Mentally and physical, make us connect in spiritual
And listen
Baby, when we do
Make all your cares invisible.
A touch can spark a million moans
Especially in the tender zones
If whispering's the cure to all that ails you
Then let me relish.
Rather, let me tell it, too
Sweet nothings by the droves
In river drops until they reach the coves.

SEEN

She stood uninvited
at the edge of my peripheral
I've never felt so grateful for intruders
Is it rude to
let my pupils dilate
to take you in
and taste the shapes
of your geometry
and watch you move
and want your choreography?
A silhouette would render me defenseless
I'd be forward if I mentioned
how your fruit inspires me to find the orchard
Is it nectar that you've tucked away
in secrets of your petals?
It's the reason all my reason
has distinguished you on pedestals
I'd love to fill the shallow of your shore
You hold me captive in the ebb and flow
of current tides
I'm drifting ever swiftly
I've reflected off your surface
could submerge into you purposely
but I respect the loyalty of buoyancy employed
I'd rather take you in with passive glance
and yearn for what's enjoyed

instead sinking vessels

Think I'd bring no anchor on the voyage

So I'll rest in here obscurity

Assure you no pursuit

as uninvited as I am

Here on the edge of your peripheral.

THOUGHTS REVEALED

No longer can restrain these thoughts
to feel you feel me physically
and orchestrate our symphony
unlyrically silently.
My lips and tongue and fingers
I promise won't behave
as your body mimics softly pounding
whispers of the waves
I tend to make you
overflow and drip
between your thighs
within your hips
you start to pour and I can
feel it when you storm
Between my sucking and my licking
and my kisses on your skin
continue drizzling and I can keep you warm
The touch we use, confuse our sense
of pleasure and of pain
as we proceed till you can't breathe without
a whisper of my name.
Wants turn into needs
and in my ears, your moans convey
that this rhythm's a necessity
our bodies clutch this way
from your collarbone to nipples

every curve and every dimple
our complexity made simple
and I'll memorize your feel
I'll kiss you 'cause you crave it
'cause I crave it's what we need
and all my thoughts will be my actions
thoughts revealed.

LOVE & MAKING (PART 1)

Love me like music that's flawless
love me like hooks and chorus
Love me like cities you visit
love me like you're a tourist
Love me like love is invincible
Indispensable
love me like it's in your memory
unforgettable
love me like harmony's natural
love me like you're an alto
Love me like intros need resolution
love me like outros
Love me like starting a revolution
love me like afro
Love me like the month of February
Like black and proud, though
Love me like rum on occasion
Love me like stimulation
Love me like you need a mental break
Not this medication
Love me like praying and holding hands
love me like stanzas
Love me like old school
Like telegrams fill empty hands
Love me like after the second chance
On a first romance

Love me like love is in body language
Love me in stance
Love me like never before this
Love me like love advanced
Love me like I've been in love with you
Like I've been entranced.

LOVE & MAKING (PART 2)

Give me my share of consideration

Give me ovations

Give me your melody

Playing loud on heavy rotation

Give me your flower

So I can give you this pollination

Give me those evenings

That we can turn into celebrations.

Give me slow rhythms and playful tussles

till we're impatient

For those contractions in pelvic muscles

What a sensation

Give me those eyes that give me those thoughts

that get me to rise

Play hard to get and then

when I get it, give me my prize

Give you positions to make you shudder

kick off the covers

Kissing your neck for those sound effects

and those silent stutters

Let's turn this lake to a waterfall

on Niagara thighs

Let's make these neighbors feel empathy

when you vocalize

Give lips and cheeks on both

Northern and Southern Hemispheres

On some I kiss or I
vanish and then I reappear
Pronounce my name while I
whisper yours in your inner ear
with heavy panting
as we reenter the atmosphere.

A TOUCH AGO

Gradually
dreaming backwards
and sleep on actions
right afterwards
honestly chose to
not think it through
desired moments
of spontaneous accidents
"So called"
So fell into fits of pleasure
Procedurally
Loving the leisure.

Compulsion
Of image.
My point of view
Gave you a dynamic.
A swing with you
In a hammock or two
Without the panic.

A lust thing official
Pro superficial
Suspended consequence
Apprehending no apprehension
Felt subtle tension

You fall in it too
Haven't we all?
Don't every one of us?
Feign guilty
Reliving the hindsight
Dishonestly
Plain sight exhilarates
Search for future excuse
But, for now,
No resonation of truth.

Sober is over
And overdone
The happenstance glance
Of something dancing
Up out a garment
Alluring but not alarming
The harm is
My subconscious
Has traded Prince Charming
For King Casual
Ruminations
Consistently vaginal.

Feeding the animalistic
Betraying the hunger

Although it lingers

Imagination

A passionate sting

I close my eyes

And awaken to

Fake reality

Mind over matter

Pardoning thoughts

I love the hazards we bring.

RIVER

Fanatically love the sound
and the feeling
When it surrounds
Profound
Even pronouncing it
gets my feet off the ground.
I'd drown
Deep in the taste
behind lace
when I'm embracing it
Slowly getting acquainted
While facing all its vibration
Painting the valley, tracing it
Laced with my salivation
Conservation of tools
Finger painting for demonstration
Rhythm consistent
Pressure is subject to fluctuation
According to sigh
According to inner thigh elevation.
Wanting rivers
A shiver from heat
A contradiction
Welcoming to this tension and
paying homage to friction
Edge of bed innovation

A celebration, I'm certain
A lover of lace but eager
For showers behind the curtain
Table manners abandoned
Your toes touching my shoulders
Then fall over conveniently
Leaning me ever closer
Greeting you as I lift
Transitioning you to edible
Soaking my soul with cultural
Utterance unforgettable
Slow-dancing my visage
Pulling for more proximity
Calling my name consistently
cancelling anonymity
Fingers climbing your slopes
I'm touching nipples at peaks
Sensation making you jerk
So strongly it makes you weak
The peach flavor I savor
You crave a talented palate
Practicing till perfection
Developing to a habit
Your perspiration is nothing
Compared to your condensation
Cause we've been using our lips
Without starting a conversation
but let me do this forever
These kisses that I deliver

Till I can see my reflection
While diving inside your river.

FULLY MOON

Truly adore the invisible you
tangible though you may be
embellished in my retelling my spectacle
Sight to behold, though you'd never wish to be held
I'm enraptured, under your spell
and your beckoning call as well
Respectable
Oh, I wish it were more than my own surmising
Warming my expectation
residing where I confide in
Horizon dweller like golden
but cool and shimmer like river
Light hearted like cirrus
I wouldn't call you a giver
you're more a doer
and taking is
making me feel I owe
I've been touching you from afar
playing ignorant when I know
and you notice nothing
while you've been my only something
I'm secretive
ever wanting the heat of your orbit
while I absorb it
consider
if I came forward

and said it's something I needed
Knowing I offer nothing
you're keeping me hot and heated
I'd face your seething rejection
There's no mistaking you mean it
daydreaming of your reflection
my very purpose depleted
so keeping you in the dark
is the safest way to consume
and dance with you in the shadows
quite lovingly
Sun and Moon.

SWEET CHAOS

Those lips grow on vines
and dance with the sun
and taunt all spring
and I can't wait till summer harvest
when they Autumn
...I mean Fall
...I mean fall for me
all in all it's a delicacy
you delicately lift golden leaves, frozen
till auburn rose gives way to forest, then bright green
A light scene in crowded memory
We shapeshift like clouds and go cumulus
You've stretched out numerous upon numerous timelines
you've asked me to catch up to your present and unwrap all
pleasantries
however, I've added hue to your complex complexion
This affection affects us relentless
This type of writer was antique, hand delivered
To hands that quivered when clicking back the buttons on your
blouse.
I've seen a trend in those lashes on eye lids.
Your eyes did maroon me on islands.
Those lashes blow hurricanes
of unspoken comprehension
compounded understanding
and unbridled unabridged narration

you side saddle on, I gallop on, you straddle on both sides of
these written lines
You've ridden
my, you're smitten by each stride
We are color outside of given lines
You've asked me to chlorophyll your margins
Excited by your Liberty cause everything green was copper first
And copper it shall be.
You've impressed upon me, wet and warm compress of paint
dressed softness
And those lips brought swelling down
I've lost for now your long forgotten evening gown
to compelling sounds of sweet chaos.

WATERCOLORR

That hesitation
you're demonstrating
Is nervousness
you're deserving of this
Elevation I offer
I'll outperform
whatever your former
wanted applauds for
much more than charm
Trust me, it's warmer do you no harm
Here in my arms
witness a calm
leave fear alone and call this place home
You know we're attracted
F how we acted
"F" for forget it all and retract it
Make something new
I know you're impacted
Pack all your things and stop living backwards
Think on these words as cure for your past
Massages and lyrical liquor—you bask in it
I'll give you more than you ask
the way we get wrapped in sheets
when we're passionate
We shake the glass in the cabinet
from what we do on counter tops

And when we climb this staircase
you climax at the very top
I cancel all the reservations you overbooked
I've read your pages
And if you bring that paperback
I'll hardcover till laminated
No pardons I get fascinated
Impressed by tangible fantasy
when I lay my head in your chest
or when that dress surrenders to gravity
We harmonize on our mental status
then jeopardize these mattresses
I dip the brush in watercolor
and make a mess on these canvases
Your fingers clutching this fabric
while I plant these kisses on clavicle
Your lips are trembling mercy, baby
I make you take a sabbatical
My longitude in your latitude
You vocalize your gratitude
You cry a little then laugh a little
I keep adjusting your attitude.

8 OFF STAGE

Sunday

Movement defines
dancing finesse of a line
Flow into shapes till they rhyme
Frozen in poses composing pictures

OFF STAGE

My present is luminescent
I guess, then,
this pen's been my best friend bar none
it's my yes-man, my henchman
My right hand, quite literally.
I write when I'm speechless
I speak more on sheets
just discrete more on beats
On these paragraphs I paraphrase
like parachutes and leap
Like I'm on stage
It's crazy
feel this stage has been on me
Man, I dream of flowing on days off
Can't wait to take this stage off
Give second thoughts to the second hand
and make it take these grays off
I used to smile in youth
when the truth was all I knew
Now the truth is ushering pain
It's heavy
my smile is broken in two
I'm more flabbergasted than sad, though
Happenstance is status quo
These wise words from I don't know
Said, "I know now, that I don't know"

Can't speak much for the future
It's never been translucent
Don't worry—when I'm silent
I probably just listened more to the music
Just got it back. I can't lose it
Confidence in His providence
He gave it to me, I use it
Consequence of His dominance
This writing thing is really just reconnaissance
That's why these words reach my soul
before they ever reach your scroll page
It's out of my control; no parole till my old age
rain, sleet, snow, this cold cage
my wingspan stays closed
I wish I reap what I sow
or is that karma status for bad actions
Give me truth with no wholes
and ask why I'm still mad at these half fractions
Been waiting long for this change
In these interactions.

TABLE OF CONTENTS

TABLE OF CONTENTS

ABOUT THE BOOK

More Than That is a compilation of poetry exploring various themes including faith, love, sex and racial tensions. The pieces are styled with a heavy emphasis on syllable placement, rhythm and rhyme scheme. Few pieces break from this norm. The author spends most of the book on musings and inner monologue, while relationship stands out as his main focus. Each chapter is introduced with a bite sized piece of poetry or two, that may or may not be related to the chapter that unfolds. *More Than That* breaks from the trends of hipster poetry, in hopes of offering more to the reader.

ABOUT THE AUTHOR

A year ago today, I would not have imagined that I would be writing to the readers of a book that I had authored . 2020 being what it has been, gave no indication that this would be a thing. Surprise seems to be the nature of poetry as far as it concerns me. For years I had felt the push and pull of poetry, towards a kind of freedom within me. I began to write at 12 years of age, and stopped abruptly at the age 19. I had experienced the end of consistent writing for 15 years outwardly, while the urge to write continued to surge within me. I do not fully know for sure, why I was unable to let the writing out. It may have been that I was afraid of the honesty that writing demanded. The fear of what others would think proved to be a halting mechanism, and a strong impediment to the art of writing. Through the undying encouragement of my friend and fellow poet Rudolph Thurman Jr., I began to take hesitant steps towards writing again, until the instinct within me revived. To this day, I honestly do not feel that I truly understand where poetry intends to take me. I do not know what it plans to take out of me. Writing feels as sporadic as a thunderstorm. I do know however, that I have loved and will love its obsession with disclosure.